THE EXTRAORDINARY LIFE OF
STEPHEN
HAWKING

PUFFIN BOOKS

UK | USA | Canada | Ireland | Australia
India | New Zealand | South Africa

Puffin Books is part of the Penguin Random House group of companies
whose addresses can be found at global.penguinrandomhouse.com.

www.penguin.co.uk
www.puffin.co.uk
www.ladybird.co.uk

Penguin
Random House
UK

First published 2019

001

Text copyright © Kate Scott, 2019
Illustrations copyright © Esther Mols, 2019

The moral right of the author and illustrator has been asserted

Text design by Jan Bielecki
Printed and bound by CPI Group (UK) Ltd, Croydon, CR0 4YY

A CIP catalogue record for this book is available from the British Library

ISBN: 978-0-241-37392-7

All correspondence to:
Puffin Books, Penguin Random House Children's
80 Strand, London WC2R 0RL

MIX
Paper from
responsible sources
FSC® C018179

Penguin Random House is committed to a
sustainable future for our business, our readers
and our planet. This book is made from Forest
Stewardship Council® certified paper.

THE EXTRAORDINARY LIFE OF
STEPHEN
HAWKING

Written by Kate Scott
Illustrated by Esther Mols

EXTRAORDINARY LIVES
PUFFIN

WHO WAS
Stephen
Hawking?

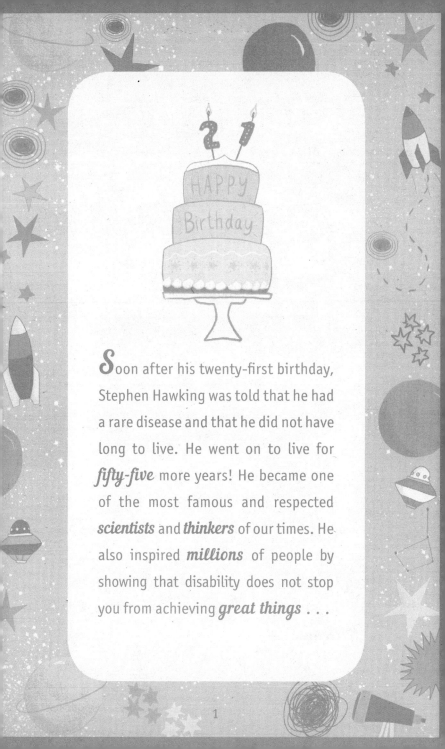

Soon after his twenty-first birthday, Stephen Hawking was told that he had a rare disease and that he did not have long to live. He went on to live for *fifty-five* more years! He became one of the most famous and respected *scientists* and *thinkers* of our times. He also inspired *millions* of people by showing that disability does not stop you from achieving *great things* . . .

STONEHENGE

CAMBRIDGE

OXFORD ST ALBANS

(HIGHGATE)

LONDON

ENGLAND

Stephen Hawking

was born in Oxford on 8 January 1942.

He went to Oxford University for his first degree and then studied at Cambridge. He was a scientist who tried to answer difficult questions, such as *'How did the universe begin?'* He definitely enjoyed a *challenge*.

Even though his condition meant that his body became increasingly weak as he grew older, Stephen's mind *remained strong* and he kept working till the end of his life. When he lost the ability to speak in 1985, a computer programmer came up with a way to help him talk using a special *speech-generating* device. This was operated by the muscles in Stephen's cheek because he could not use his mouth or hands to type.

On to the next challenge!

Did you know?
Stephen experienced a zero-gravity flight when he visited the Kennedy Space Center in 2007.

Stephen Hawking was in a *wheelchair* for most of his life, but this did not stop him travelling *all over the world*.

During his life Stephen Hawking published many books. The most famous of them was called *A Brief History of Time*. It sold more than **ten million** copies. He won many awards for his work and was celebrated across the world in a variety of ways.

Let's look more closely at the **extraordinary** life that he led . . .

Stephen's beginnings

Stephen's father, *Frank*, came from a long line of farmers in Yorkshire, but he became a doctor after going to Oxford University. Stephen's mother, *Isobel*, came from Scotland, and her family moved to Devon when she was twelve. She went to Oxford University too.

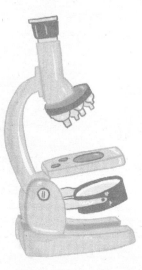

Did you know?
Isobel was from a large family – she was one of eight children.

Frank Hawking regularly travelled to Africa to research **tropical diseases** as part of his work. Isobel worked as a tax inspector, but she didn't like that job at all. She later became a medical research secretary, which is how she met Frank. They married in 1941.

WORLD WAR II

During the Second World War (which ended in 1945), the Germans agreed not to bomb Oxford or Cambridge. The British in return agreed not to bomb two cities in Germany. That made Oxford a much safer place to have a baby.

Stephen Hawking was born in Oxford in 1942, even though at the time his family lived in Highgate in London.

Stephen was the *first child* born in his family. Eighteen months later his sister *Mary* was born. He wasn't very happy to have a sister at first! His sister *Philippa* was born when Stephen was almost five and by that time Stephen was more used to the idea of having a sibling. When Stephen was fourteen his parents adopted a boy called *Edward*.

Did you know?
Stephen Hawking was born exactly 300 years after the death of Galileo, an incredibly important Italian astronomer, physicist and philosopher.

GALILEO GALILEI

First memories

Stephen Hawking's first memory was not a very happy one. He remembers being two and a half, crying and crying in the nursery of Byron House School. He was upset because he wanted to play with the other children but was too *frightened* to join in.

Did you know?
Stephen Hawking did not learn to read until he was eight years old.

The Second World War had not yet ended when Stephen Hawking was born. Once, when he and his sister were out with their mother, a V-2 ROCKET landed just a few houses away from their home in *Highgate*. His father was at home but luckily he was not hurt.

V-2 ROCKET: a long-distance missile.

The explosion meant that for years afterwards there was a bombsite close by. Stephen used to *play* there with a friend who lived a few doors away from him. After the war ended it was quite common for bombsites to become like adventure playgrounds to local children.

When Stephen Hawking was a child, he loved model trains. What he wanted more than anything else was an *electric train*.

This was not easy to get because even after the war toys were hard to come by. During the war, food was RATIONED, and treats like toys were not seen as important. Many of the factories that usually made toys now had to make things like guns for use in the war.

Stephen was given a wooden train that was made by his father and then two *clockwork* trains sometime after that, but none of them worked very well. So one day Stephen decided to do something about his problem himself. When his parents were out, he took out money from his Post Office bank account and spent it on an *electric train*!

WHAT IS RATIONING?

During the Second World War, a lot of Britain's food came from other countries (as it still does today). It was transported on ships. These ships were regularly targeted and sunk by the enemy. Rationing was introduced to make sure people got a fair share of the food that was available because there wasn't much to go around. Everyone was given a book of coupons. When you paid for your shopping, you had to give one of your coupons too, and once you had used up your 'ration' for that particular food (for example, cheese or meat) then you could not buy any more that week.

When Stephen Hawking was about eight years old, his family moved from London to the nearby city of St Albans. Their new house needed lots of *repairs* before they moved in. Stephen's father Frank worried about how much it would cost to get other people to work on the house, so he tried to do it all himself. Unfortunately Frank wasn't very good at it!

Frank found it hard not to ***worry*** about money, even when he had a good job and a steady income. This meant that he tried to ***save money*** in whatever ways he could. When Stephen was growing up, his father decided that they did not need central heating in the house, so the house was often very cold. Frank's solution to this was to wear lots of jumpers and a dressing gown over his normal clothes!

In the new house, Stephen's room was one of the rooms that a servant might have slept in, if the family had servants. Because of this, it had a bell that could be rung from the kitchen.

Stephen wanted that room specifically because it was possible to *climb out* of the window on to the roof of a shed and then down to the ground, so he could come and go as he liked!

Life growing up

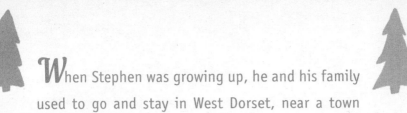

When Stephen was growing up, he and his family used to go and stay in West Dorset, near a town called **Weymouth** on the coast. They would stay in a *caravan* that Stephen's mother and father had bought and painted green.

Stephen and his sisters slept inside the caravan on bunk beds his father had made, and their parents slept in a tent alongside it.

One year, when Stephen was about eight years old, Stephen's father went away for four months so that he could **research** tropical diseases. Isobel decided to take her children to visit a friend in Mallorca, Spain. This was not a simple journey at the time because Spain was under the DICTATORSHIP of Francisco Franco, who had been an ally of Hitler and Mussolini during the Second World War. Going by plane wasn't possible, so the journey was much more difficult than it would be today and involved taking a **boat** and a train.

DICTATORSHIP: when a single group or person (who is not a king or queen, or elected) has absolute power and is in charge of a country.

FRANCISCO FRANCO

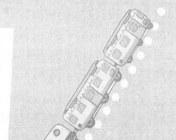

LONDON

ENGLAND

PARIS

FRANCE

LYON

SPAIN

BARCELONA

VALENCIA

MALLORCA

While they were in Mallorca, Stephen had lessons with the tutor of their friend's son. However, the tutor wasn't very interested in teaching the two boys – he was too busy writing a play!

Did you know?
Stephen had very untidy handwriting when he was a child.

A couple of years later, Stephen took the ELEVEN-PLUS EXAM (though he was only ten when he took it). Having passed the exam, he went to St Albans School, where the children were separated into different streams. You had to do well in all your *tests* to stay in the top group. Stephen just about managed to stay in the *top stream*.

ELEVEN-PLUS EXAM:
an exam taken by some children in the UK to determine which secondary school they will go to.

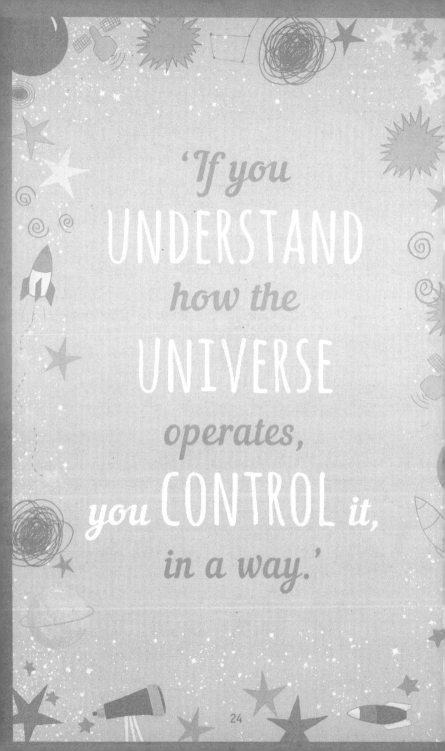

'If you **UNDERSTAND** *how the* **UNIVERSE** *operates,* *you* **CONTROL** *it,* *in a way.*'

When Stephen was in his teens, he **invented** lots of games with a school friend. He also spent quite a lot of time **building** model boats and planes (although he said that he wasn't very good at it!). Later in life, Stephen reflected that the reason he liked creating games and building things was probably because he wanted to know *exactly* how things worked.

Stephen had several good *friends* at St Albans and stayed in touch with them for the rest of his life. They talked about all kinds of things – including wondering how the universe began.

Did you know?
Stephen Hawking was nicknamed 'Einstein' by his classmates!

'When I was twelve, one of my friends BET ANOTHER FRIEND a bag of sweets that I would never COME TO ANYTHING. I DON'T KNOW if this bet was ever settled, AND IF SO, which way it was decided.'

Because Stephen's father spent a lot of time researching tropical *diseases*, he had his own laboratory and kept an INSECT HOME as part of his work.

INSECT HOME:
a man-made place to house insects and keep them alive.

Stephen loved visiting his father's laboratory and looking through the microscope, but he always felt a little *nervous* because there would be mosquitoes flying about!

'I was always
very interested in
HOW THINGS OPERATED
and used to
TAKE THEM APART
to see
HOW THEY WORKED.
But I was not so good at
PUTTING THEM BACK
together again.'

Choosing his
subject

Frank Hawking hoped that his son would follow him into *medicine*, but Stephen wasn't interested in biology.

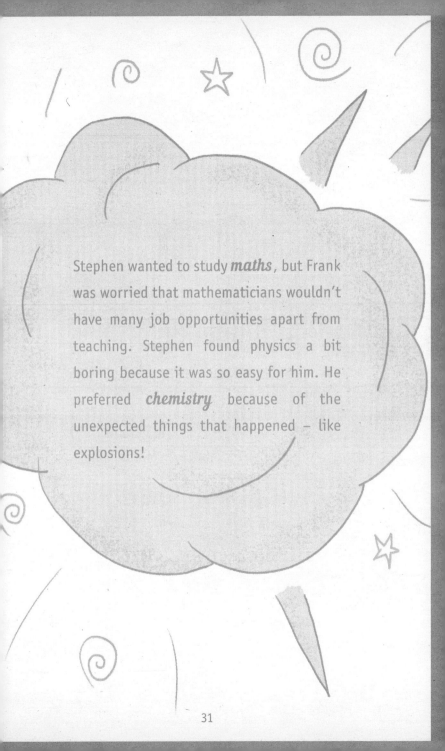

Stephen wanted to study *maths*, but Frank was worried that mathematicians wouldn't have many job opportunities apart from teaching. Stephen found physics a bit boring because it was so easy for him. He preferred *chemistry* because of the unexpected things that happened – like explosions!

University

Stephen ended up choosing to study **physics** and **chemistry**. He took a scholarship exam for Oxford University when he was only seventeen years old. His family had gone to live in India for a year but Stephen stayed behind to take his A levels and the scholarship *exam*.

After his exams, he travelled to India and spent the summer holidays there. It was quite an *adventure*. They were there during the rainy season and the car that his family had brought over from Britain had to be towed over some roads that had been partly washed away!

'*Stephen always had* A STRONG SENSE OF *wonder* AND I COULD SEE THAT *the stars* WOULD DRAW HIM.'

– Stephen's mother, Isobel

Stephen was convinced he had done badly in his university entrance exams, but when he came home at the end of the summer he received a telegram offering him a *scholarship*.

Did you know?

Although Stephen started university early, it was quite common at the time for some students to be much older than others. For some years after the war many people had to do MILITARY SERVICE and so their studies were delayed.

MILITARY SERVICE: working in the armed forces.

Stephen went to university a year earlier than most people, so he felt quite lonely when he first started at University College, Oxford.

One of the ways Stephen Hawking made new friends was by joining the Oxford University Boat Club as a COXSWAIN. Stephen wasn't very lucky, though. In his very first race the boat went *off course* and his team were DISQUALIFIED.

WHAT IS A COXSWAIN?

In rowing, a coxswain is in charge of the crew of a boat. They make sure that the boat is going in the right direction and that everyone rowing is going as fast and smoothly as they can. The cox is the coach and the leader during races, shouting out instructions and encouragement.

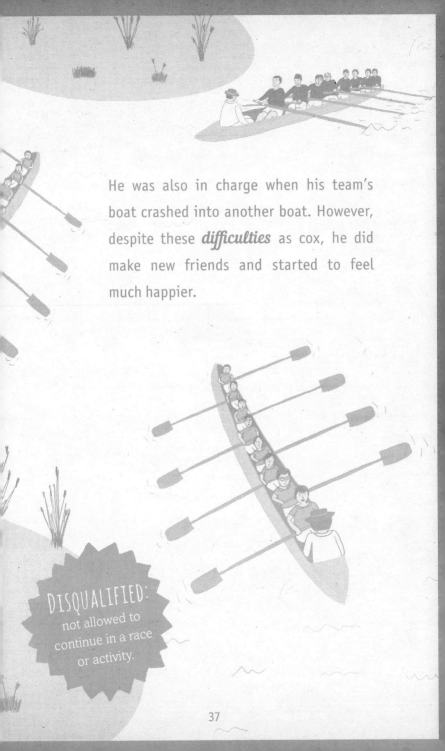

He was also in charge when his team's boat crashed into another boat. However, despite these *difficulties* as cox, he did make new friends and started to feel much happier.

DISQUALIFIED:
not allowed to continue in a race or activity.

Travels

Stephen Hawking's college offered students special GRANTS so that they could travel abroad. Stephen applied for one of the grants and used the money to go to Iran with a friend in 1962.

GRANT:
money given or gifted to a person (usually by a large organization) without it needing to be paid back.

The two friends travelled first by train and then by bus. They shared their bus with lots of **chickens** and sheep. It must have been quite noisy (and a bit smelly too).

The trip turned out to be even more eventful than Stephen could have imagined. On the way home, he was ill while riding in a bus along the very rough roads. The bus was *bouncing* about so much that Stephen didn't realize that they were actually in the middle of an *earthquake*.

The earthquake was very serious – over 12,000 people died. Even though it was a major earthquake, Stephen and his friend didn't know it had happened until days later. At the time, there were no mobile phones or computers to make it easy and quick to be in touch with family. Stephen's parents were left waiting for *ten days* before they knew he was safe. Stephen was lucky – his only injury was a broken rib.

When Stephen was in the *final year* of his degree at Oxford, he fell down some stairs. He realized he had been becoming quite *clumsy* and was worried enough to go to a doctor. The doctor wasn't concerned and thought Stephen's clumsiness might have been from drinking too much alcohol.

Cambridge

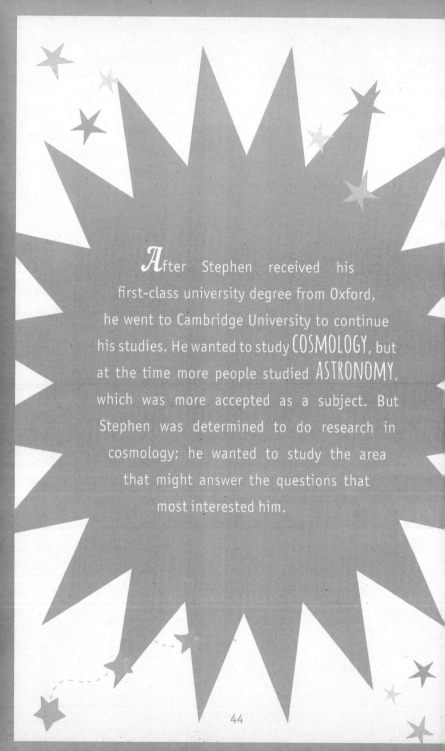

$\mathcal{A}$fter Stephen received his first-class university degree from Oxford, he went to Cambridge University to continue his studies. He wanted to study COSMOLOGY, but at the time more people studied ASTRONOMY, which was more accepted as a subject. But Stephen was determined to do research in cosmology; he wanted to study the area that might answer the questions that most interested him.

WHAT IS ASTRONOMY?

Astronomy is the study of space, planets and the physical universe.

WHAT IS COSMOLOGY?

Cosmology is the study of how the universe began. It is a combination of astronomy and particle physics.

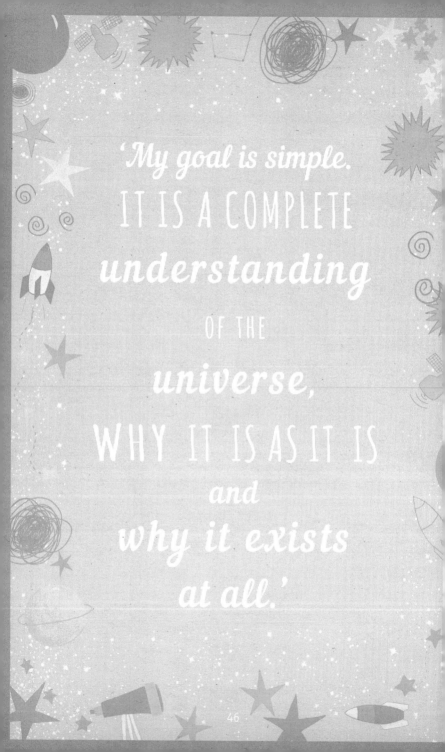

'My goal is simple.
IT IS A COMPLETE
understanding
OF THE
universe,
WHY IT IS AS IT IS
and
why it exists
at all.'

46

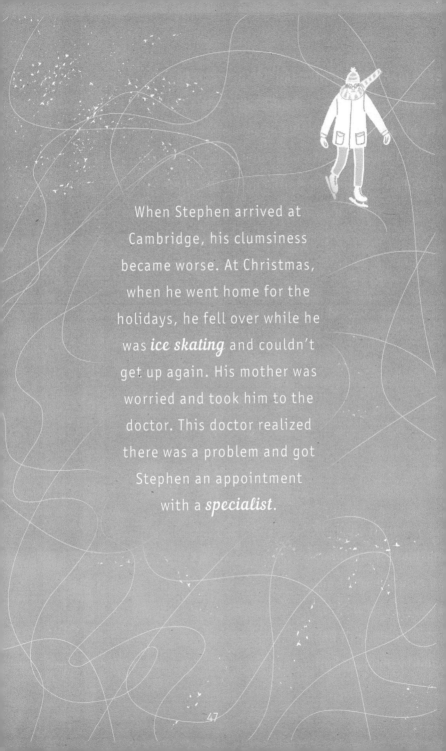

When Stephen arrived at Cambridge, his clumsiness became worse. At Christmas, when he went home for the holidays, he fell over while he was *ice skating* and couldn't get up again. His mother was worried and took him to the doctor. This doctor realized there was a problem and got Stephen an appointment with a *specialist*.

A testing time

Soon after Stephen's twenty-first birthday, he went into **hospital** to have lots of different tests. He had to stay in hospital for two weeks. It was a worrying time for both Stephen and his family. At the end of all the tests, the doctors told him that they expected him to get **worse**, not better – though they couldn't tell him what was wrong. They also said there was nothing they could do except give him vitamins.

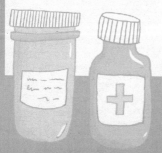

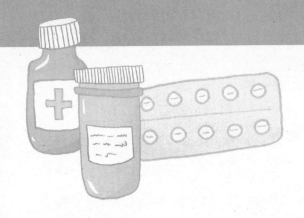

When Stephen did find out what was wrong, he was shocked and upset to discover that he had an incurable disease: MOTOR NEURONE DISEASE. The doctors told him that he wasn't likely to live for more than *a few years*. They told him to carry on with his work. Understandably Stephen found this very difficult to do at first.

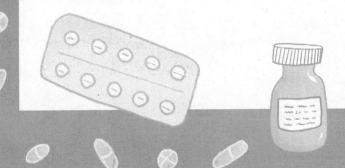

WHAT IS
MOTOR NEURONE DISEASE?

Motor neurone disease (MND) is
also known as amyotrophic lateral
sclerosis (ALS) or Lou Gehrig's
disease. It is a rare illness that affects
the brain and nerves (motor neurons).
Over time, the cells stop working.
No one knows why this is. As the
disease progresses, the body becomes
increasingly weak. There is no cure,
but there are treatments that can help
people cope with the disease day to
day. Early signs can be weakness in
the legs, difficulty holding things and
talking, weight loss, muscle cramps
and twitches.

After Stephen had had time to get used to the idea of having the disease, he began to be *determined* not to give in to it.

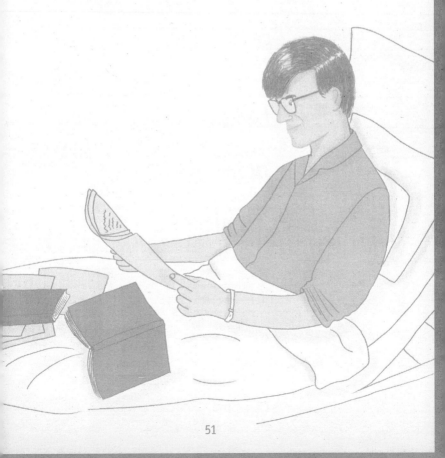

'Before my condition
WAS DIAGNOSED,
I had been very bored
WITH LIFE . . .
But . . . I suddenly realized
that there were a lot
OF WORTHWHILE THINGS
I could do.'

Carrying on

Stephen Hawking found himself wanting to *work harder* than he ever had before.

Stephen had also fallen in love with *Jane Wilde*, whom he met through a mutual friend. Finding out he might not have long to live made him want to make the most of life for as long as possible.

His disease made things difficult for him, but Stephen was **determined** to find solutions to the problems. When it became too hard for him to write or type, he would ask someone to write down his thoughts as he spoke them and then type them up for him. This meant he was able to produce work that **impressed** the other scientists and professors despite the physical problems he was facing.

WE ARE JUST AN ADVANCED BREED OF MONKEYS ON A MINOR PLANET OF A VERY AVERAGE STAR.

Receiving a RESEARCH FELLOWSHIP meant that Stephen and Jane could afford to get *married*. By the time of their marriage, Stephen needed a *stick* to walk.

RESEARCH FELLOWSHIP: when a university pays someone to do research in their subject.

Over the next five years, Stephen and Jane had two children: *Robert* and *Lucy*. They also travelled in the United States of America because of Stephen's work. It was sometimes hard for Jane; she not only had their children to look after but her husband too. This could be exhausting as well as worrying.

Black holes and the Big Bang

Stephen wanted to tackle the biggest question in cosmology at the time: *did the universe have a beginning?* Some scientists didn't like the idea that the universe had started at a particular point in time and argued against it. Stephen thought, along with some others, that there was evidence that the universe did have an *exact starting point.* It was an exciting period for Stephen as very few people were working on this question.

WHAT IS A BLACK HOLE?

A black hole is a place in space where particles of matter have been squashed so tightly together, and the pull of gravity is so strong, that nothing can get through – not even light.

What is the 'Big Bang'?

The Big Bang is a theory that the universe started from a state of extremely high temperature and density – just tiny particles, which grouped together to form atoms. Eventually atoms combined to form stars and galaxies.

Stephen had started to lose the use of his limbs, but he did not let this stop him from working. Instead of writing out **equations**, he taught himself to **visualize** things in his mind. Some people think this new way of working might even have helped him come up with his theories.

$$E = mc^2$$

$$\frac{1}{c^2} \frac{d^2 \phi_n}{\partial t^2} - \nabla^2 \phi_n + \left(\frac{mc}{\hbar}\right)^2 \phi_n = 0$$

$$T_H = \frac{\hbar c^3}{8 \pi G k_B M}$$

$$S = \frac{\pi A k c^3}{2 \hbar G}$$

The concept of **black holes** had been around for over **200** years, ever since a man called John Michell put forward his idea of what he called **'dark stars'** in 1783.

JOHN MICHELL

In order to prove that the **beginning of the universe** had come about with some sort of 'big bang', Stephen Hawking had to first work on the idea of black holes. Stephen realized that the **maths** he had used to prove the existence of black holes could also be used to prove the existence of the **Big Bang**. This work is part of what would lead Stephen Hawking to be known around the world.

California

*I*n 1974, aged thirty-two, Stephen Hawking was elected to be a Fellow of the Royal Society. This was a very great honour, especially for someone who was so young. Soon afterwards, he was invited to *California* to work at the California Institute of Technology (Caltech). By this point, Stephen had been using a wheelchair for several years, as well as an electric three-wheeled car.

Did you know?
Stephen Hawking sometimes gave people lifts in his three-wheeled car, even though it was illegal!

In California, Stephen and his family were able to enjoy luxuries such as *colour television*, which was still unusual back in Britain. The children loved living in California.

Physical changes

$\mathcal{S}$tephen and Jane had their third child, Timothy, in 1979. In the years after Timothy was born, Stephen's **health** became much worse. He began to have long choking fits and in 1985, on a trip to Switzerland, Stephen developed **pneumonia**. It was one of several points when doctors feared Stephen would not recover.

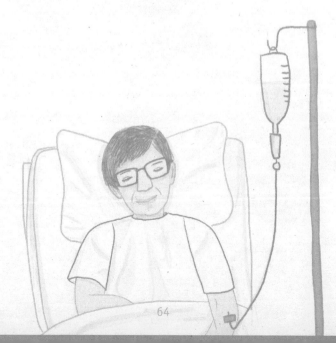

His wife Jane insisted that he was flown back to Britain and there Stephen got better – but only after the hospital in Cambridge had performed an *operation* that meant that Stephen could no longer speak. Although before this his speech had become slurred, now he was not able to talk at all. The only way he could *communicate* was to raise his eyebrows when someone pointed to the right letter on a card and spell words out letter by letter.

OK   A

G

B

'IT IS PRETTY DIFFICULT TO *carry on a* **conversation** LIKE THAT, LET ALONE *write a* SCIENTIFIC *paper.'*

M

YES

NO

3

A man called Walt Woltosz in California created a special SPEECH SYNTHESIZER for Stephen.

SPEECH
SYNTHESIZER:
a machine that
creates artificial
speech

The synthesizer ran on a small personal computer. Stephen could either *speak* or *save* his words on to a disk. He could also print his words out on to paper so that he could speak in *sentences* once he had them stored up. (If he tried to speak in real time, the program could only manage around *three* words a minute. If you try this yourself, you will realize that it is quite slow.) Later, when more 'natural-sounding' synthesizers became available,

Stephen decided to keep the same voice because by then people *recognized* the sound of his artificial voice. Stephen operated the voice synthesizer by using the *muscles* in his cheek.

'MY MAIN INTERFACE
TO THE COMPUTER
IS THROUGH AN
OPEN SOURCE PROGRAM . . .

*This provides a
software keyboard
on the screen.*

A CURSOR AUTOMATICALLY
SCANS ACROSS THIS KEYBOARD
BY ROW OR BY COLUMN.

*I can select a character
by moving my cheek
to stop the cursor.'*

A Brief

History of

Time

$\mathcal{S}$tephen became increasingly **worried** about how much longer he could survive. He decided to write a **book** about his work in the hope that it would help support his family.

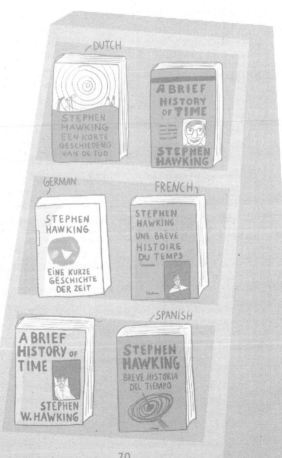

'I want my books
SOLD ON
AIRPORT BOOKSTALLS.'

Stephen wanted his book to be something that *anyone* could read, even if they were not a scientist and had only a basic knowledge about the subject. For this reason he chose a publisher known for popular books (the kind sold at airports!). Stephen's editor helped him make his book something that most people would be able to understand. This was not an easy task because the ideas were very **complicated**.

Stephen managed to
do what he set out to do. *A
Brief History of Time* was published
in 1988 and soon became *a bestseller*.
It has been translated into more than
thirty-five *languages* and sold
more than ten million copies.
It was the beginning of
Stephen Hawking's *fame*.

Changes at home

*T*he strain of Stephen's health over the years led Stephen and Jane to decide to divorce in 1995. They remained friends and both of them **remarried**.

Stephen Hawking had a number of **health scares** in the following years but each time he managed to get through them. His second wife, Elaine, who was a nurse, in some cases **saved his life**. But after a number of years together they too divorced and Stephen lived with a housekeeper for the rest of his life. Jane, his first wife, lived nearby with her second husband.

Did you know?

Stephen Hawking was well known for his sense of humour. In 1995 *The Face* magazine asked Stephen Hawking if he had an equation for time travel. This was his reply: 'I do not have any equations for time travel. If I did, I would win the National Lottery every week.'

Work and disability

While Stephen Hawking's disease made his life *difficult* in many ways, it also proved that disability does not prevent a person from achieving great things. Stephen even thought that in some ways he was able to achieve so much *because* of his condition.

'*I have been able to devote myself completely to research.*'

'I have had a
FULL
AND
satisfying
LIFE . . . I HAVE
managed to do
MOST THINGS
I WANTED.'

Stephen Hawking was also able to capture the world's imagination partly because of his disability. People wanted to know his *story*. They were impressed by the efforts he made to overcome the effects of his illness to explore some of the biggest *questions* in science. He was also an inspiration to other people with disabilities.

Stephen Hawking *travelled* widely. He visited every continent apart from Australia – including Antarctica.

In 2007 Stephen Hawking went to the Kennedy Space Center in the United States and experienced a *zero-gravity flight*.

'The smile on his face . . . would have moved the stars.'

– Jane Wilde

Popular culture

Stephen captured the public imagination and, as a result, not only were television shows and films made *about* him, but he also appeared on television himself. He **presented** many programmes about his work, and he also enjoyed appearing in some very unexpected shows.

For example, in several episodes of *The Simpsons* he voiced himself. He sometimes joked that people thought he was a *Simpsons* character! Stephen also appeared in another **cartoon** show called *Futurama*, where he was a fiercer version of himself – in one episode he even shot **lasers** from his eyes!

Another television programme he appeared in was the US sitcom *The Big Bang Theory* – and of course Stephen had done lots of theorizing about the Big Bang himself. He found the show very funny and agreed to appear in **seven episodes**. Stephen also appeared in an episode of *Star Trek*, which seems appropriate since space travel was another of his passionate interests.

Did you know?
In 2002, after a UK-wide vote, the BBC included Stephen Hawking in their list of 100 Greatest Britons.

Did you know?

In 2009 Stephen Hawking threw a party for time travellers. He did not send out the invitations until after the party. He decided that if guests had showed up, it would prove that time travel was real. Unfortunately no one turned up so he decided that it wasn't possible (yet)!

WELCOME, TIME TRAVELLERS

In 2004 a television film called *Hawking*, starring Benedict Cumberbatch, was made about Stephen Hawking's life. Then in 2014 a *feature film* called *The Theory of Everything* was released, starring Eddie Redmayne and Felicity Jones. It was about Stephen's *relationship* with his first wife, Jane (the film was based on a book by her).

With his daughter, Lucy, Stephen wrote a series of *children's books* about adventures in space and time – the first of which is called *George's Secret Key to the Universe*.

Using his fame to inspire

Stephen spoke at the 2012 Paralympic Opening Ceremony. He wanted to use his position as a famous scientist to help **promote and support** the study of science. He was also passionate about trying to make people understand what science could make possible, and what we are capable of ourselves.

In 2015 and 2017 Stephen Hawking appeared in comedy sketches for COMIC RELIEF, using his fame to help raise money for good causes.

COMIC RELIEF: a major charity in the UK that works towards creating a world free from poverty.

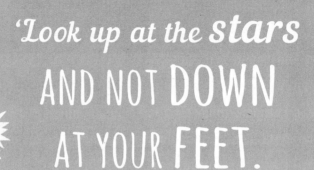

'Look up at the **stars**
AND NOT DOWN
AT YOUR FEET.
Try to make sense
OF WHAT YOU SEE,
and **wonder** *about what*
MAKES THE UNIVERSE EXIST.
Be curious . . .'

As well as the many *scientific awards* that Stephen Hawking received during his life, he has been recognized in other ways too. His contribution to science has been celebrated by having *museums* and buildings named after him. There is a Stephen W. Hawking science museum in San Salvador, El Salvador; the Stephen Hawking Building in Cambridge; and the Stephen Hawking Centre at the Perimeter Institute in Canada.

An Extraordinary Life

On 14 March 2018 Stephen Hawking died at the age of *seventy-six*, fifty-five years after he was told he did not have long to live. He himself had not expected to live for so long.

'*My expectations were reduced to zero when I was twenty-one. Everything since then has been a bonus.*'

'*I'm happy*
IF I HAVE ADDED
something to our
UNDERSTANDING
of the *universe*.'

Most of all, he helped millions of people understand how our world works – and how much more there is to find out.

TIMELINE

1942
Born in Oxford on 8 January.

1950
Moved from Highgate to St Albans.

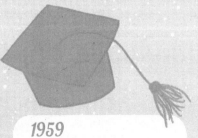

1959
Won a scholarship to Oxford University.

1962
Graduated with a
first-class degree and
began his research in
cosmology at the
University of Cambridge.

1963
Diagnosed with an 'incurable disease',
later discovered to be motor neurone
disease (MND).

1965

Completed his PhD at the age of twenty-three and married Jane Wilde (and went on to have three children with her: Lucy, Robert and Timothy).

1974

Appointed Fellow of the Royal Society.

1977
Appointed Professor of Gravitational Physics at Cambridge.

1979
Appointed Lucasian Professor of Mathematics at Cambridge.

1982
Awarded a CBE by the Queen.

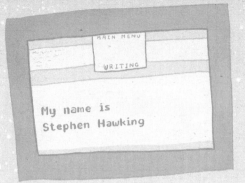

My name is
Stephen Hawking

1985

Lost the ability to speak.
A computer programmer
invented a synthesized voice
program for him to use.

A BRIEF
HISTORY OF
TIME

STEPHEN
W. HAWKING

1988

Published *A Brief History of Time:
From the Big Bang to Black Holes*.

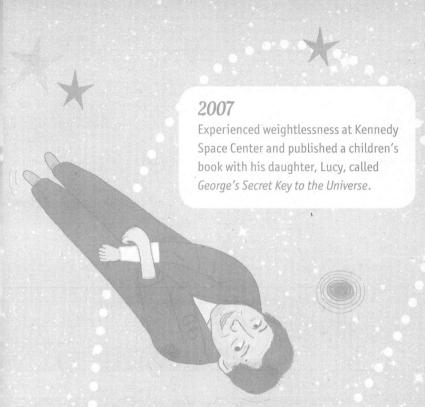

2007
Experienced weightlessness at Kennedy Space Center and published a children's book with his daughter, Lucy, called *George's Secret Key to the Universe*.

1995
Divorced from Jane Wilde and married Elaine Manson.

2009
Awarded the US Presidential
Medal of Freedom.

2013
Awarded the Fundamental Physics Prize
(accompanied by prize money of $3 million dollars).

2014
The Theory of Everything, a film about
Stephen Hawking and his first wife, was
released.

2015
Announced a project to search for extra-terrestrial intelligence with billionaire Yuri Milner.

2018
Died in Cambridge, England, on 14 March, at the age of seventy-six.

SOME THINGS TO THINK ABOUT...

Stephen Hawking wanted to make a difference to the world. How do you think he felt when he first found out about his incurable disease?

If time travel became possible in your lifetime, where would you travel to?

The future?

Or the past?

Why?

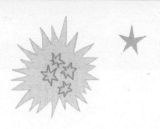

There are still so many exciting things to learn about our universe. Can you imagine what else might be out there, ready to be discovered?

Index

amyotrophic lateral sclerosis (ALS) 50

Big Bang 58, 60, 81
The Big Bang Theory 81
black holes 57, 60
A Brief History of Time 4, 69–72

California 62
cosmology 44–46, 56–60

Galileo 8

Hawking, Edward 8
Hawking, Frank 6, 15–17, 20, 27, 30–31
Hawking, Isobel 6, 20, 34
Hawking, Lucy 55, 84
Hawking, Mary 8
Hawking, Philippa 8
Hawking, Robert 55
Hawking, Stephen
    birth and childhood 2, 8–28
    A Brief History of Time 4, 69–72
    California 62
    Cambridge 43–47
    choosing his degree subject 29–32
    cosmology 44–46, 56–60
    death 88
    disability 1, 3, 42, 47–55, 59, 62,
    64–68, 73, 75–77
    and Elaine 73
    family 6
    and Jane 53, 55, 73
    popular culture 79–81, 84
    sense of humour 74
    and time travel 74, 82–83
    timeline 94–101
    travels 39–41, 77
    university 32–37
    using his fame to inspire 85–87
    zero-gravity flight 3, 78

Hawking, Timothy 64
Hawking (film) 84

India 33

Lou Gehrig's disease 50

Mallorca 20–22
Manson, Elaine 73
Michell, John 60
motor neurone disease (MND) 50

Second World War 7, 10–11, 12, 13
St Albans School 23–25
Simpsons, The 80
Star Trek 81

The Theory of Everything 84

Wilde, Jane 53, 55, 73, 78, 84
Woltosz, Walt 66

Quote Sources

Direct quotes throughout are from *My Brief History* by Stephen Hawking (2013), except the below:

Page 34: 'Stephen Hawking's Scottish mum Isobel – and how she was the first to predict his scientific greatness' (*Daily Record* article by Lisa Toner and Aoife Moore, 14 March 2018)

Page 46: *Stephen Hawking's Universe* (by John Boslough, 1985)

Page 68: 'My Computer' on the official Stephen Hawking website (www.hawking.org.uk/the-computer.html)

Pages 71, 88: 'The Science of Second-Guessing' (*New York Times* article by Deborah Solomon, 12 December 2004)

Page 86: Stephen Hawking's speech at the Paralympic Opening Ceremony, Olympic Stadium, London, 2012

READ MORE BOOKS BY
Stephen and Lucy
Hawking . . .

LUCY & STEPHEN HAWKING

GEORGE'S SECRET KEY TO THE UNIVERSE

Like a Doctor Who adventure
Sunday Times

LUCY & STEPHEN HAWKING

GEORGE'S COSMIC TREASURE HUNT

What would you do if an alien
got in touch?

LUCY & STEPHEN HAWKING

GEORGE AND THE UNBREAKABLE CODE

George and Annie are heading out of
this world to save the universe!

LUCY & STEPHEN HAWKING

GEORGE AND THE BIG BANG

Going back to the beginning
of time

LUCY & STEPHEN HAWKING

GEORGE AND THE BLUE MOON

Like a Doctor Who adventure . . . inspiring
curiosity and amazement *Sunday Times*

LUCY HAWKING

GEORGE AND THE SHIP OF TIME

Like a Doctor Who adventure . . . inspiring
curiosity and amazement *Sunday Times*

She became an inspiration all over the world
when she stood up for everyone's right to an
education. Turn the page for a glimpse of

THE EXTRAORDINARY LIFE OF

MALALA
YOUSAFZAI

WHO IS
Malala
Yousafzai?

Malala Yousafzai

was born on 12 July 1997, in the beautiful
Swat Valley in the north of Pakistan.

One afternoon, she boarded the school bus with her friends, discussing the exam questions. It was a hot and humid day.

But then two young men appeared, and everything changed.

They leaned into the bus and wanted to know which girl was Malala.

When they found her, they shot her. She was unconscious before she reached the hospital.

Have you ever wondered what it takes to become one
of the most influential women in the world? Find out in

THE EXTRAORDINARY LIFE OF

MICHELLE
OBAMA

Read on for a sneak peek . . .

Michelle at school

Michelle went to Bryn Mawr Elementary School in Chicago. By the time she was eleven years old she was on a programme for *gifted and talented students*, where she learned French and biology. When she went to high school she joined America's first state-funded 'magnet' school, Whitney M. Young Magnet High School, which had *special courses* designed to attract certain students like a magnet.

Whitney M. Young High School is open to all Chicago students, but entrance is based on good grades and entrance exam performance. Michelle was admitted because she was a *brilliant student*, but it did mean that she had to travel for over two hours every day in order to attend.

'For me,
EDUCATION
was power.'

▶◀ X · X ▶◀ · ●)) · ▶◀ X · X ▶◀ · ●)) ·

Whitney M. Young High School
was named after Whitney M. Young,
a civil rights leader whose work involved
breaking down barriers of inequality and
segregation for African Americans.

▶◀ X · X ▶◀ · ●)) · ▶◀ X · X ▶◀ · ●)) ·

Michelle was fully **qualified** at twenty-five years old, and Barack was a twenty-seven-year-old law student. They were two of only a few black people who worked at Sidley Austin at the time.

Michelle had promised her mother that she would concentrate on her work, and not dating!

Their **professional relationship** started in 1989, with business meetings, lunches with clients, and community organization meetings. But then Barack asked Michelle on a date! She politely said no, because at first she didn't think it was **appropriate** to date him because she was his mentor. As time went on, though, she realized she liked him too, despite her initial thought that he had a big nose!